Developing Double-Stops

for VIOLIN

A Complete Course of Study for Double Note and Chord Development

The study of double-stops constitutes one of the most important phases of technical training on the violin. Students everywhere have found difficulty in playing double-stops, particularly *thirds* and *octaves*. This is due partly to a neglect in practicing these intervals enough, and again, due to practicing them in an improper fashion. Often double-stops are not introduced in violin study until students are preparing for *Kreutzer*, or actually studying these celebrated caprices. Unfortunately, students introduced at this late stage to the intricacies of playing two or more tones simultaneously are seriously handicapped, for they have no basic technic with which to support their advanced endeavors. Usually such students, when encountering double-stops in advanced materials, struggle through them in a highly unsatisfactory manner, and before long are quite ready to consider the feat of playing two or more tones simultaneously a phase of technic quite beyond their reach.

Sound pedagogy demands that the study of double-stops be introduced early in violin training; in fact, such study should be commenced as soon as students have completed any one of the many standard first year violin texts. The first double-stops taken up should be *sixths* because they are the easiest intervals to play in tune on the violin; next, *thirds*, *octaves* and *chords* (compound double-stops) should be studied. *Tenths* and *fingered octaves* should not be introduced until students are physically capable of making the stretches demanded of them in executing such advanced types of finger technic.

Before actually playing two tones simultaneously, students should play them as broken intervals, or one tone after the other. Following this procedure, double-stop exercises should be played in a manner referred to by the author as "prepared double-stops," that is, each tone played separately, and then together as a combined unit. The purpose of these preliminary steps is to enable students to hear pitches individually, and thus establish correct finger positions before attempting to combine them into a harmonic interval.

Students will discover, when attempting to play *thirds* and *octaves* and finding them out of tune, that the trouble usually is in the lower tone, and if the finger producing that tone is adjusted slightly, the interval becomes properly in tune. Most students, in playing double-stops, and finding them out of tune, attempt to correct the matter by exerting more pressure on the bow. Obviously, this will not remedy the situation at all; instead, students must adjust their fingers until they fall in the proper place on the fingerboard. In the playing of regular *octaves* (not *fingered octaves*), some teachers advise students, for reasons of security, to keep their third finger down, in addition to the first and fourth fingers, unless playing in positions higher than the seventh. It is quite clear that as the higher positions are reached, the fingers fall closer together, and as a result it becomes virtually impossible to include the third finger in the grasp of the hand as it approaches the end of the fingerboard. In the matter of double-stop shifting, students must shift forward on the fingers that were last down, and likewise shift backward on the fingers that were last down.

The present work, which constitutes a complete course of study in the art of double-stop and chord playing, is so graded that it may be used in conjunction with any violin method or series of etude books. The material presented in the early pages of the work is easy enough to be studied upon the completion of any beginner's book, and as the course of study progresses, it reaches a stage of advancement comparable to the famous etudes of *Kreutzer*, *Fiorillo* and *Rode*. For those ambitious students who complete the present volume, and are in quest of material for additional double-stop study, the author recommends the diligent practice of two and three octave scales in *thirds*, *sixths*, *octaves*, *fingered octaves* and *tenths*. For those who complete the present course of study, and then heed the advice given above, there is the assurance of a complete mastery of the art of double-stop playing.

Harvey S. Whistler, Ph. D.

Developing Double-Stops in the First Position
Sixths

BROKEN SIXTHS ON A AND E STRINGS

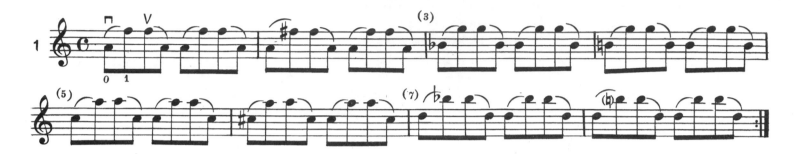

PREPARED SIXTHS ON A AND E STRINGS

BROKEN SIXTHS ON D AND A STRINGS

PREPARED SIXTHS ON D AND A STRINGS

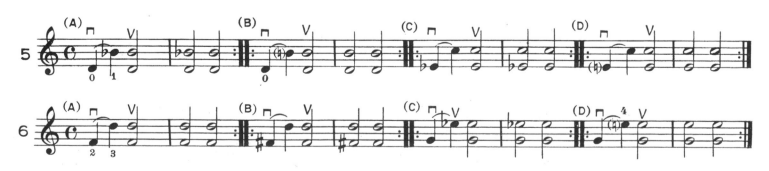

Copyright MCMXLVII by Rubank, Inc., Chicago, Ill.
International Copyright Secured

BROKEN SIXTHS ON G AND D STRINGS

PREPARED SIXTHS ON G AND D STRINGS

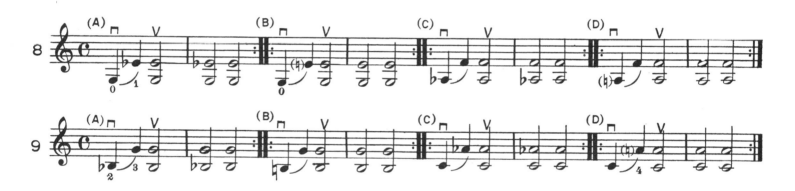

EXERCISES IN SIXTHS

Thirds

BROKEN THIRDS ON A AND E STRINGS

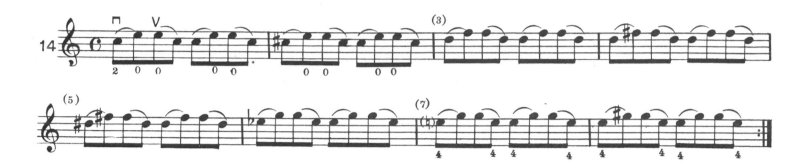

PREPARED THIRDS ON A AND E STRINGS

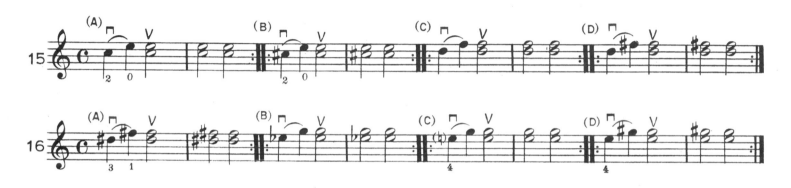

BROKEN THIRDS ON D AND A STRINGS

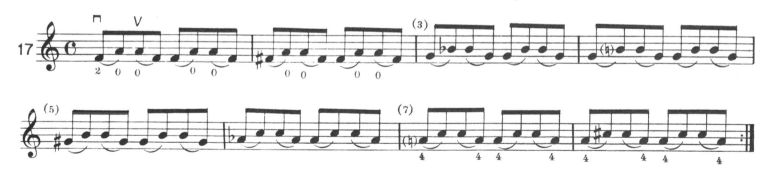

PREPARED THIRDS ON D AND A STRINGS

BROKEN THIRDS ON G AND D STRINGS

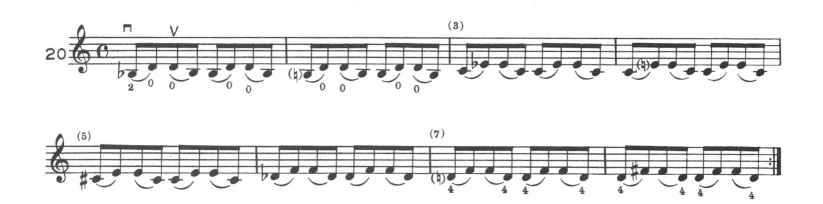

PREPARED THIRDS ON G AND D STRINGS

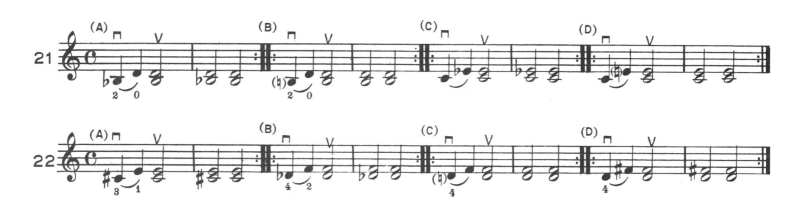

EXERCISES IN THIRDS

Octaves

BROKEN OCTAVES ON A AND E STRINGS

PREPARED OCTAVES ON A AND E STRINGS

BROKEN OCTAVES ON D AND A STRINGS

PREPARED OCTAVES ON D AND A STRINGS

BROKEN OCTAVES ON G AND D STRINGS

PREPARED OCTAVES ON G AND D STRINGS

Fourths

BROKEN FOURTHS ON A AND E STRINGS

PREPARED FOURTHS ON A AND E STRINGS

BROKEN FOURTHS ON D AND A STRINGS

PREPARED FOURTHS ON D AND A STRINGS

BROKEN FOURTHS ON G AND D STRINGS

PREPARED FOURTHS ON G AND D STRINGS

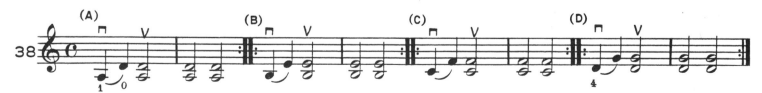

Single-Stops and Open Strings

E AND A STRINGS

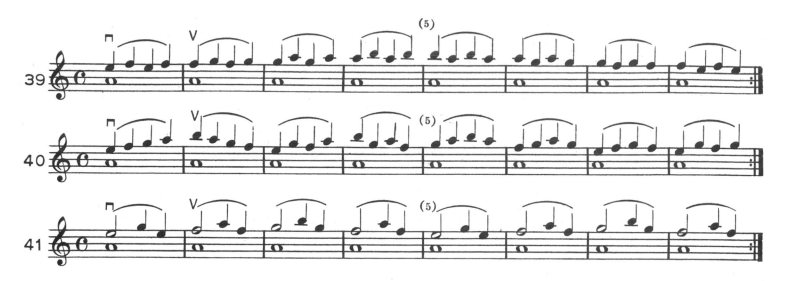

A AND D STRINGS

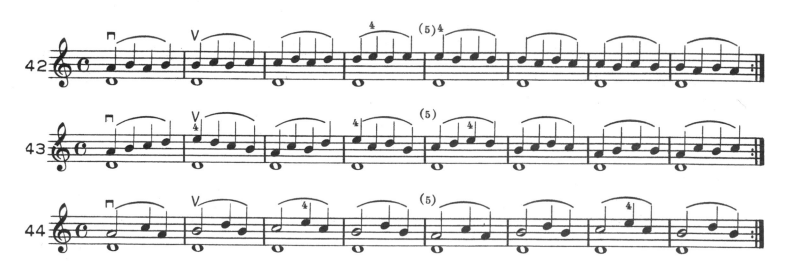

D AND G STRINGS

A AND E STRINGS

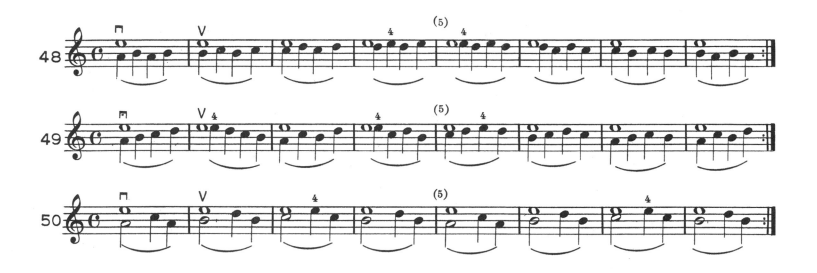

D AND A STRINGS

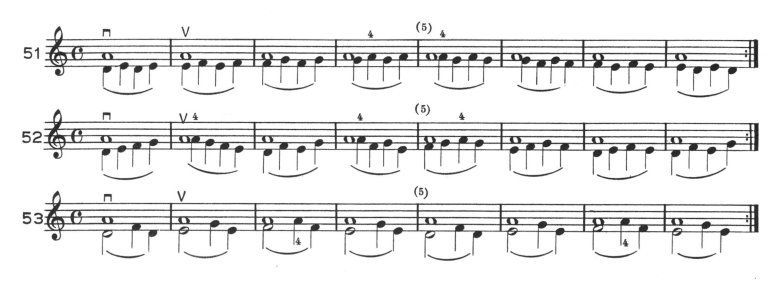

G AND D STRINGS

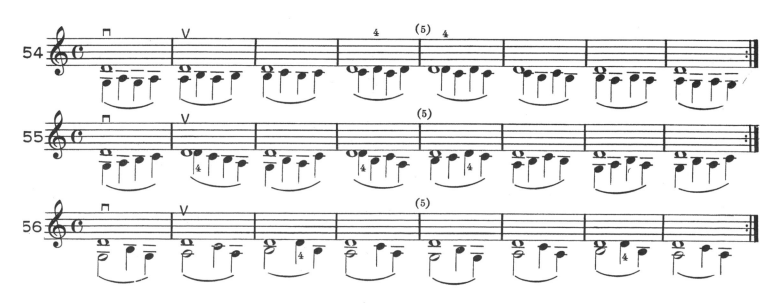

Exercises in Prepared Double-Stops

SIXTHS

THIRDS

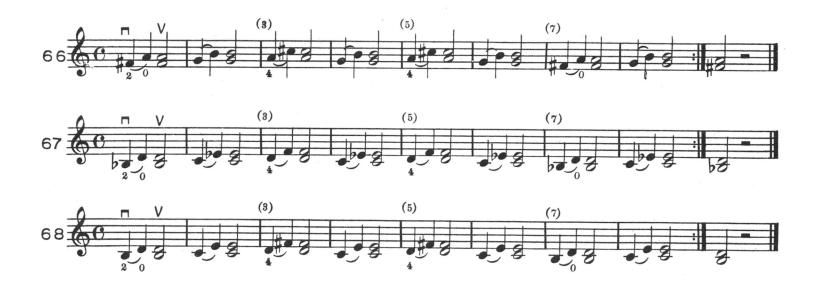

OCTAVES

FOURTHS

11

Double-Stop Technic Builders

Developing Chords in the First Position
THREE-NOTE CHORDS

When playing three-note chords, first play the lower and middle tones together, immediately tilting the bow, and playing the middle and upper tones together. Gradually, the tones of three-note chords may be played simultaneously.

FOUR-NOTE CHORDS

When playing four-note chords, first play the lower two tones together, immediately tilting the bow and playing the upper two tones together.

DOUBLE-STOP STUDIES IN THE FIRST POSITION

Etude No.1 in C

SITT

Etude No.2 in C

SITT

Etude in G

SITT

Etude in B♭

SITT

Serenade

SCHUBERT

DOUBLE-STOP DUET IN THE FIRST POSITION

Canzonetta

WICHTL

Developing Double-Stops in the Third Position

E AND A STRINGS

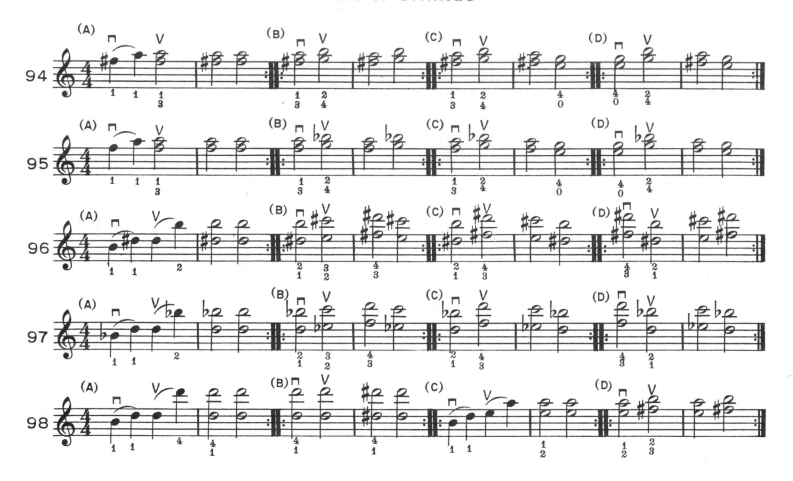

A AND D STRINGS

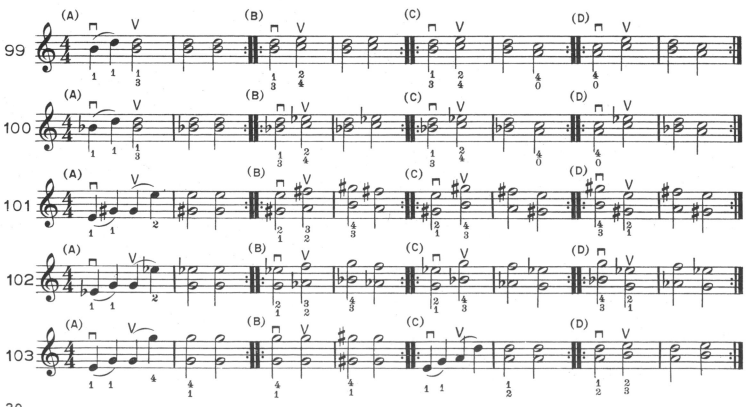

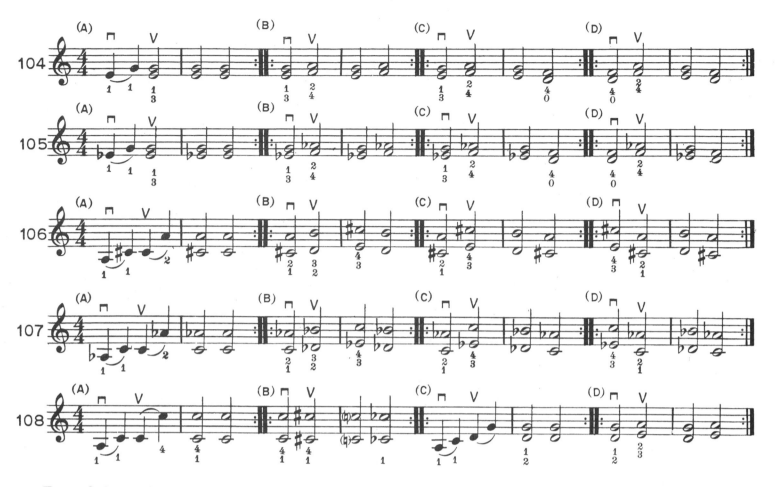

Double-Stop Shifting Between First and Third Positions

Also practice using a separate bow for each interval.

Shifting with Changes of Fingering

The student should shift forward on the fingers that were last down, and likewise, shift backward on the fingers that were last down.

The small notes in the following exercises indicate the movement of the fingers in shifting, and as the student perfects his ability to shift from one note to another, the small notes eventually should not be heard.

THIRDS

Also practice using a separate bow for each third.

TECHNIC BUILDERS

DEVELOPING SCALE PASSAGES

DOUBLE-STOP ETUDE IN THE FIRST AND THIRD POSITIONS

Etude in Sixths

De BERIOT

DOUBLE-STOP SOLOS IN THE FIRST AND THIRD POSITIONS
Hungarian Dance No.V

BRAHMS

Wedding March
FROM A MIDSUMMER NIGHT'S DREAM

MENDELSSOHN

DOUBLE-STOP DUET IN FIRST AND THIRD POSITIONS

Eventide

SPOHR

Chord Study in the First and Third Positions

De BERIOT

Developing Double-Stops in the Second Position

E AND A STRINGS

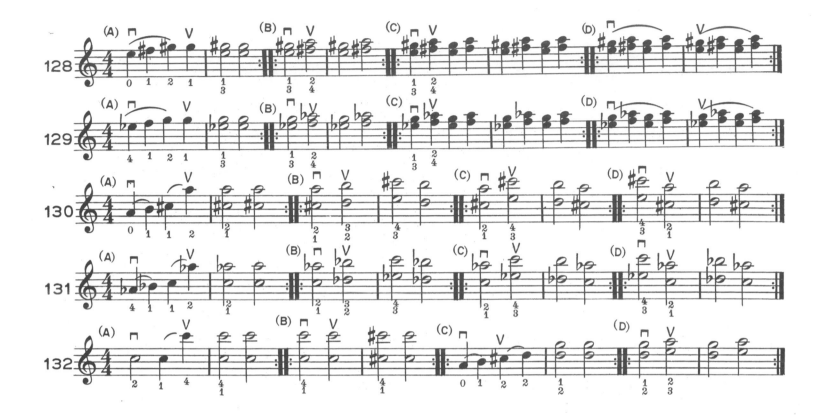

A AND D STRINGS

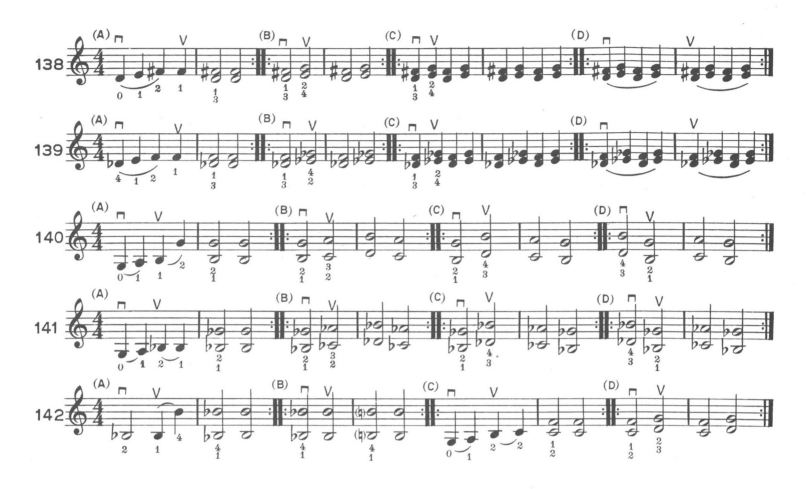

Double-Stop Shifting Between First and Second Positions

Also practice using a separate bow for each interval.

DOUBLE-STOP ETUDES IN THE FIRST, SECOND AND THIRD POSITIONS

Etude in F

SITT

Etude in A

SITT

DOUBLE-STOP DUET IN THE FIRST, SECOND AND THIRD POSITIONS

Nocturne

De BERIOT

Developing Double-Stops in the Fourth Position

E AND A STRINGS

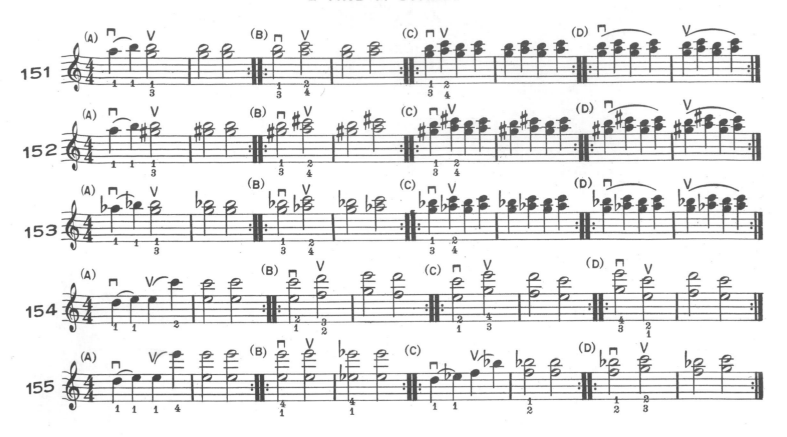

A AND D STRINGS

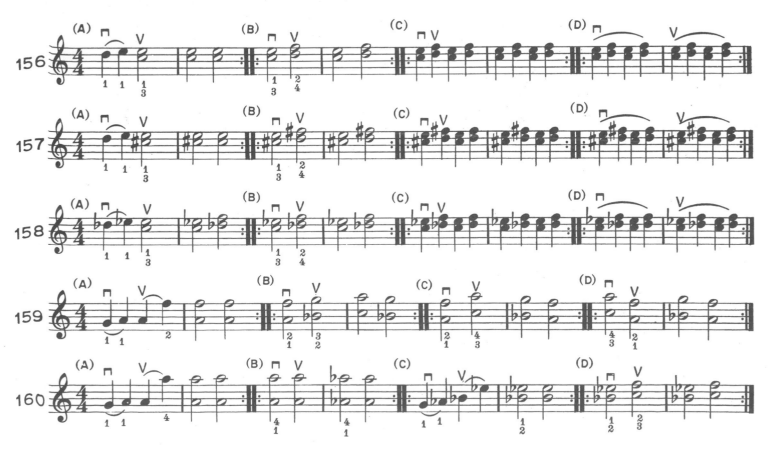

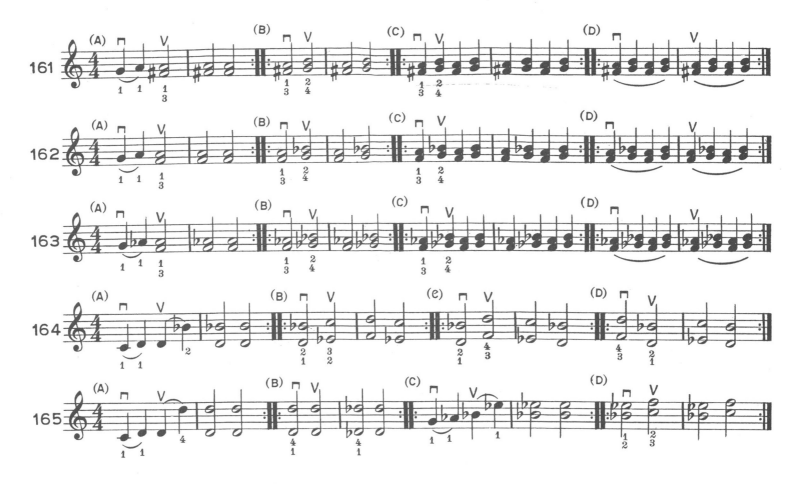

Double-Stop Shifting Between Third and Fourth Positions

Also practice using a separate bow for each interval.

Developing Double-Stops in the Fifth Position

E AND A STRINGS

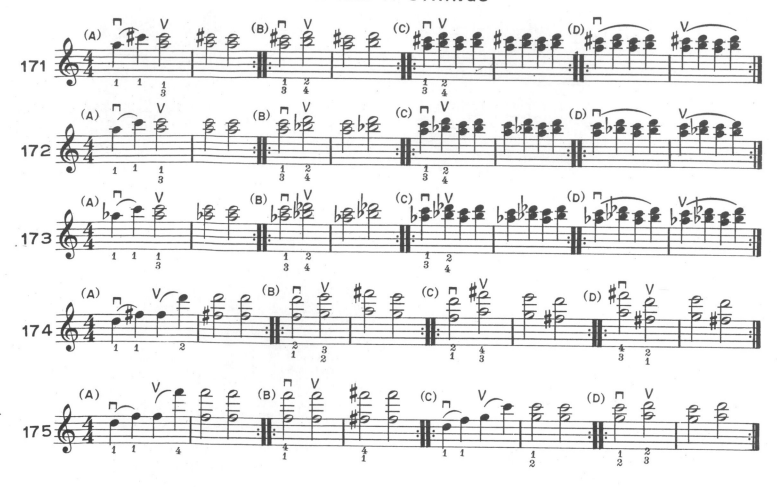

A AND D STRINGS

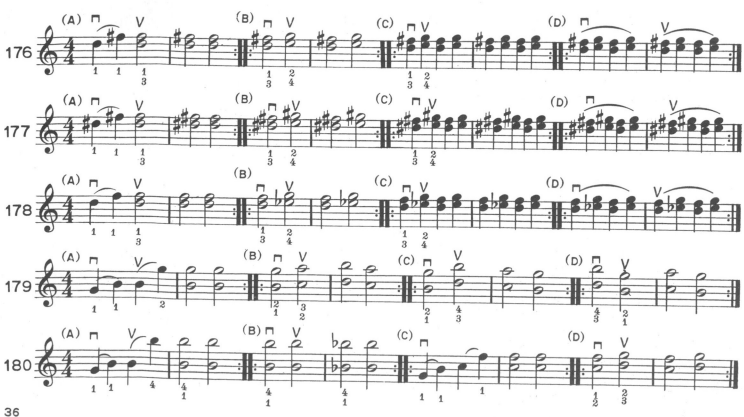

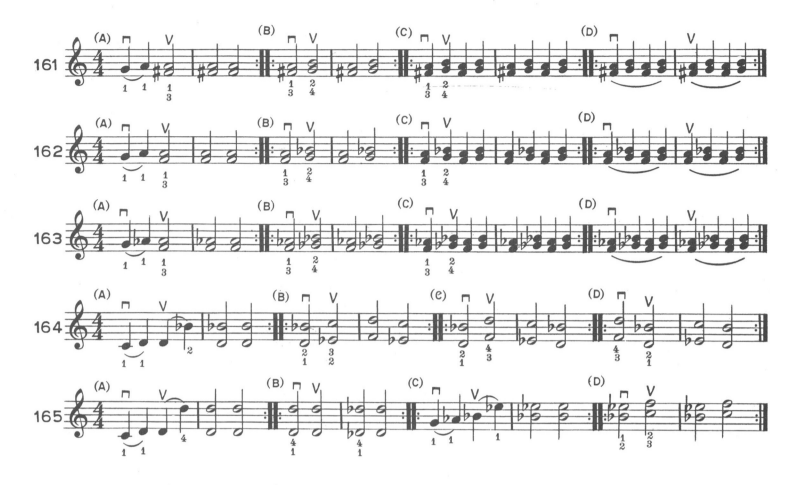

Double-Stop Shifting Between Third and Fourth Positions

Also practice using a separate bow for each interval.

Developing Double-Stops in the Fifth Position

E AND A STRINGS

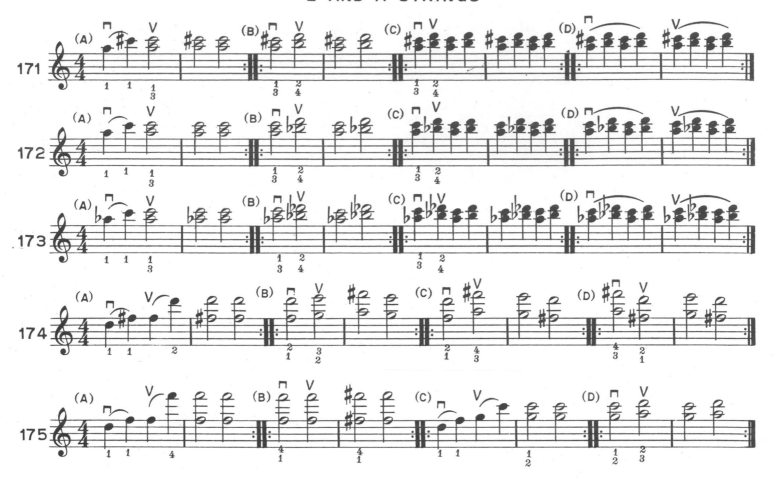

A AND D STRINGS

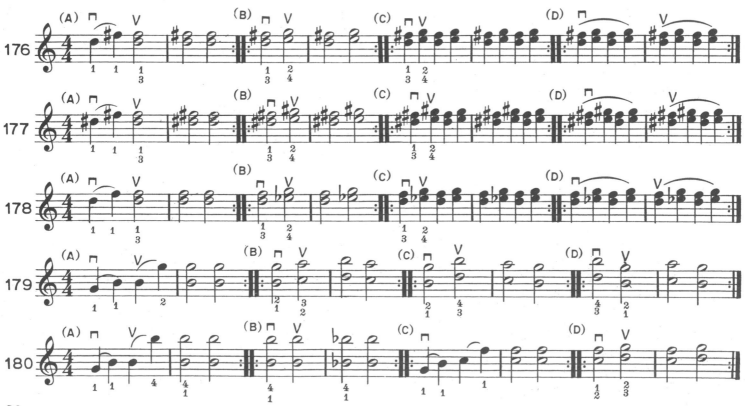

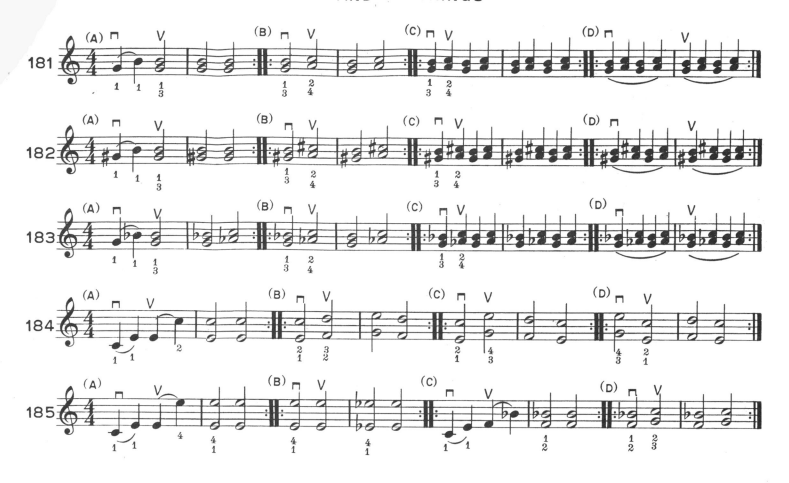

Double-Stop Shifting Between Third and Fifth Positions

Also practice using a separate bow for each interval.

Advanced Double-Stop Shifting

SHIFTING BETWEEN SECOND AND THIRD POSITIONS

Also practice using a separate bow for each interval.

SHIFTING BETWEEN SECOND AND FOURTH POSITIONS

Also practice using a separate bow for each interval.

SHIFTING BETWEEN FOURTH AND FIFTH POSITIONS

Also practice using a separate bow for each interval.

CHROMATIC SHIFTING

Also practice (1) using a separate bow for each sixth and (2) slurring each two sixths.

VIRTUOSO SHIFTING

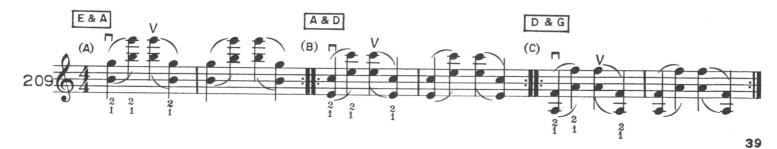

Advanced Shifting with Changes of Fingering

The student should remember to shift forward on the fingers that were last down, and likewise, to shift backward on the fingers that were last down.

The student also should remember that the small notes in the following exercises indicate the movement of the fingers in shifting, and as the ability to shift from one note to another is perfected, the small notes eventually should not be heard.

THIRDS

Also practice using a separate bow for each third.

TECHNIC BUILDER

DEVELOPING SCALE PASSAGES

DOUBLE-STOP ETUDE IN FIVE POSITIONS

Etude in G

BLUMENSTENGEL

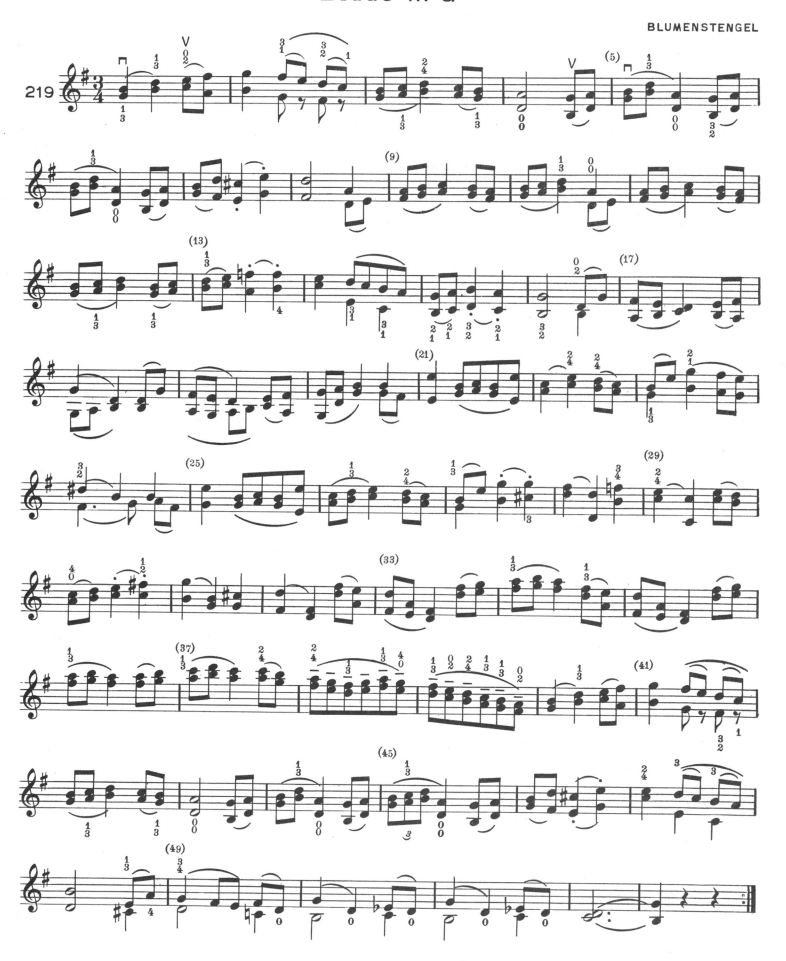

Developing Octaves

Prepared Octaves in the First Three Positions

Keep 1st, 3rd and 4th fingers on strings except when playing open string and 3rd finger.

Prepared Octaves in the First Five Positions

Octaves in the First Three Positions

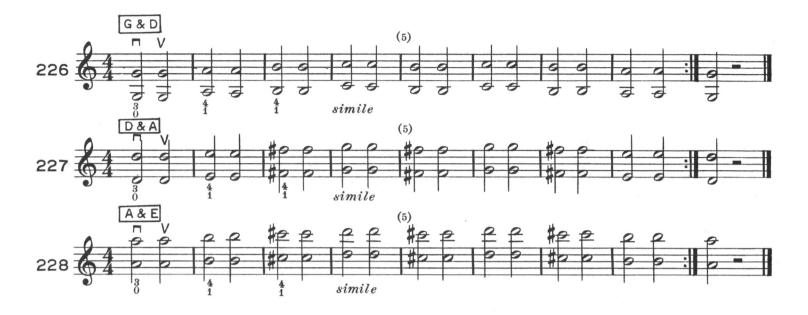

Octaves in the First Five Positions

Chromatic Study in Prepared Octaves

Chromatic Study in Octaves

Also practice slurring the two octaves within each measure.

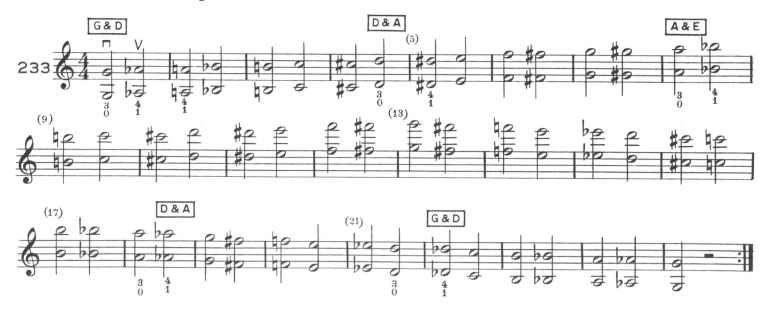

Diatonic Study in Prepared Octaves

Diatonic Study in Octaves

Also practice slurring the two octaves within each measure.

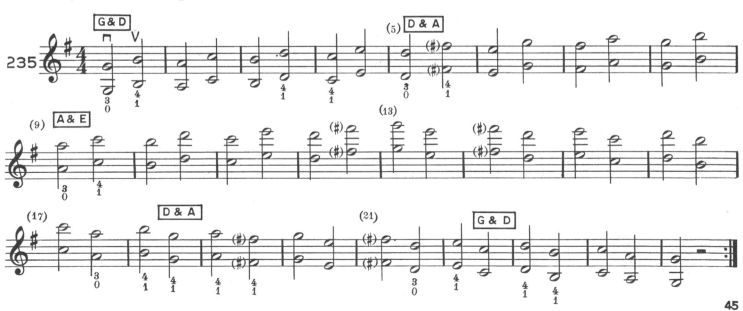

Etude in Prepared Octaves

LEONARD

Etude in Prepared Octaves

ALARD

Etude in Octaves

Etude in Octaves

ALARD

Introduction to Scales in Octaves

Also practice each scale in prepared octaves.

Bowings to be practiced:

Mastery of Octaves

(A) In developing a complete mastery of octaves, the player will find it necessary to practice each of the following chromatic exercises. These should be played from memory. Play the exercises in both prepared octaves and straight octaves.

(B) Also practice the following exercises (1) slurring each two tones, and (2) slurring each four tones.

Valse-a-la-Octaves

De BERIOT

Introducing Fingered Octaves

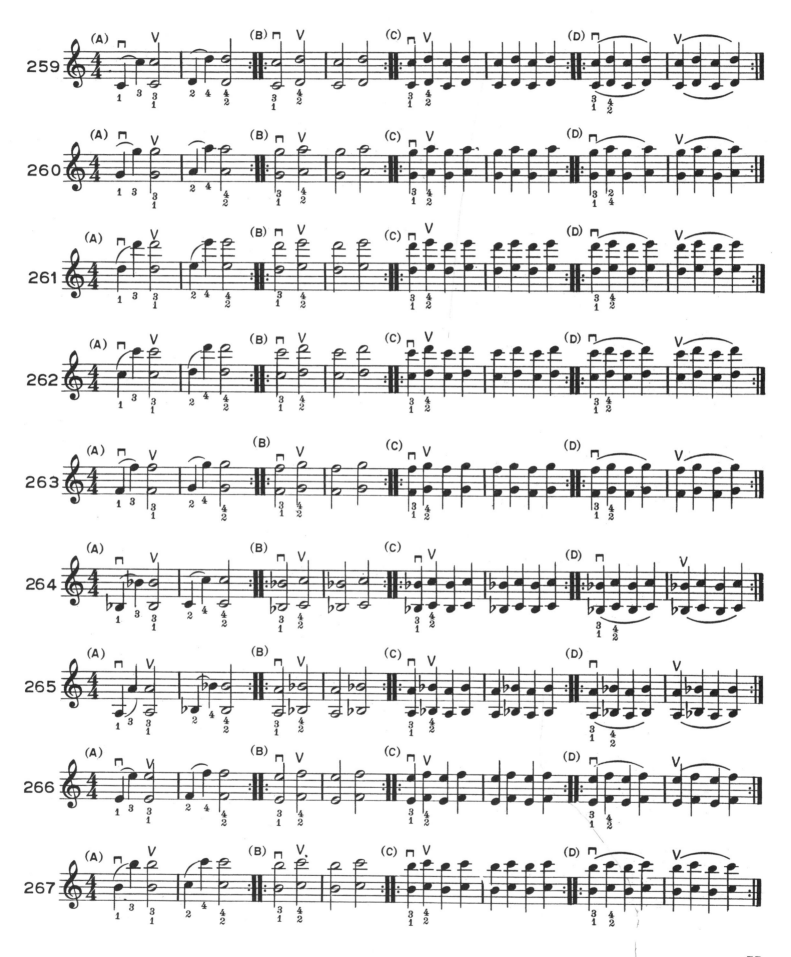

Preparing Scales in Fingered Octaves

Fingered Octave Scale Passages

Also practice (1) slurring two tones, (2) slurring four tones, and (3) slurring eight tones.

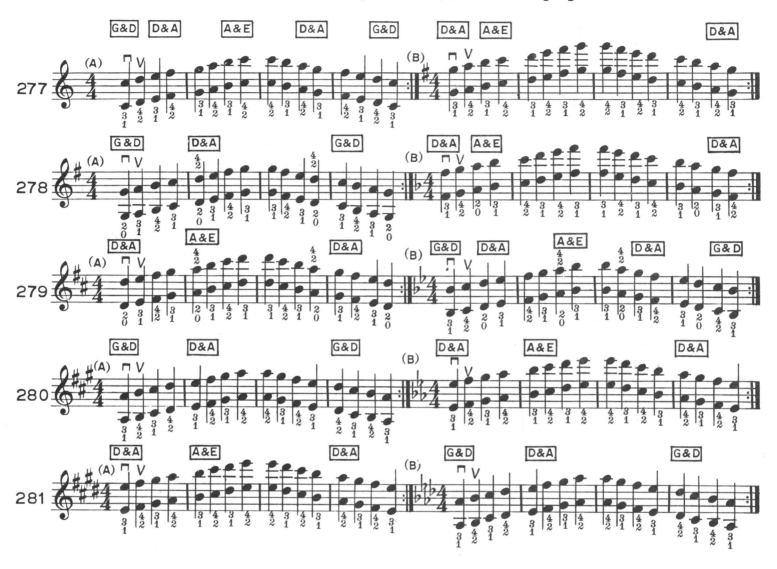

Strengthening Fingers with Fingered Octaves

Practice slowly. Strike fingers forcefully on the fingerboard.

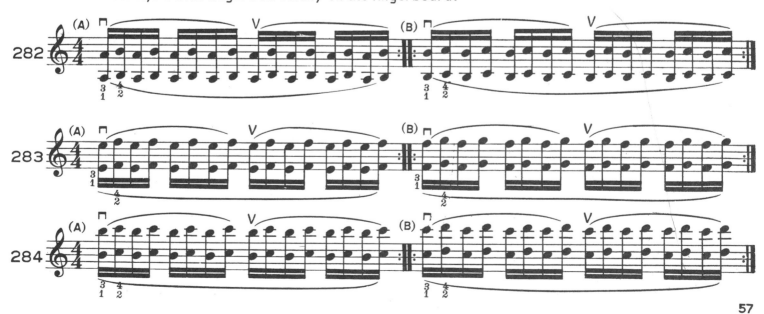

Developing Thirds

Ascending Foundation Studies in Thirds

Also practice using a separate bow for each third.

Descending Foundation Studies in Thirds

Also practice using a separate bow for each third.

Introduction to Scales in Thirds*

Bowings to be practiced.

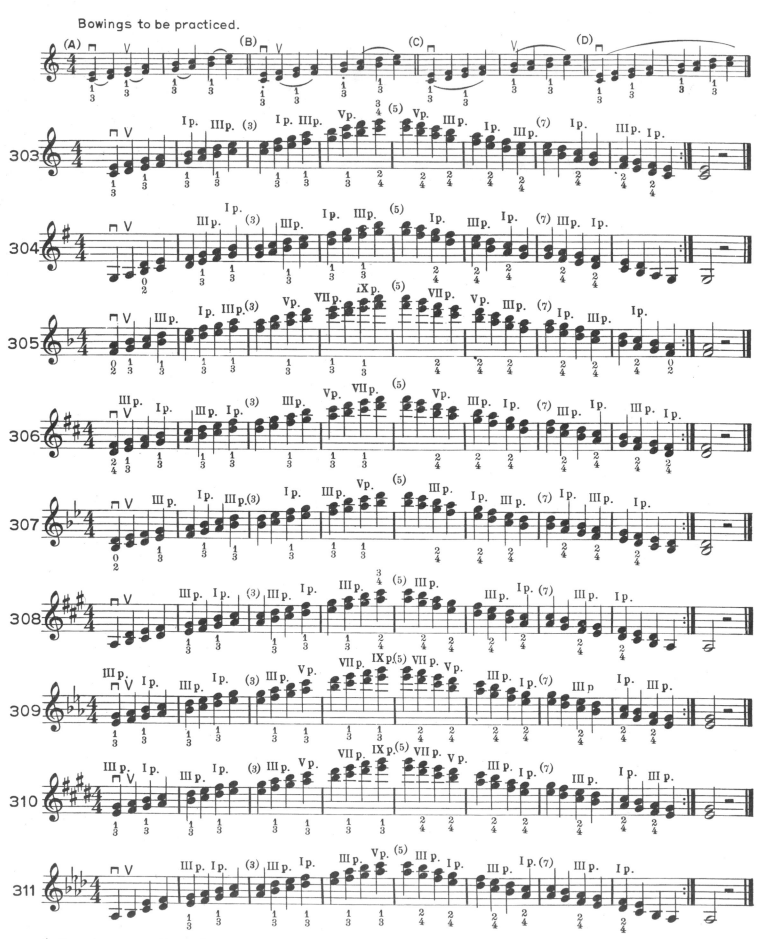

* Fingerings are optional. Teachers should substitute their own fingerings when they are better suited to their needs.

60

Introduction to Scales in Sixths*

Bowings to be practiced.

* Fingerings are optional. Teachers should substitute their own fingerings when they are better suited to their needs.

Interval Review

De BERIOT

Developing Tenths

BROKEN TENTHS

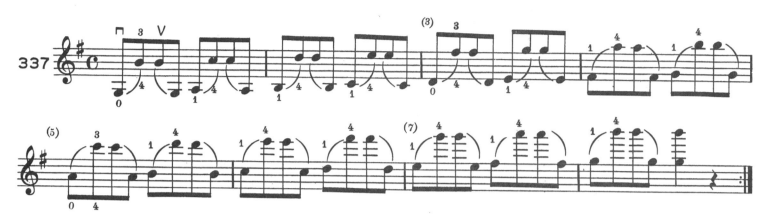

PREPARED TENTHS
(Stretching Fourth Finger Forward)

PREPARED TENTHS
(Stretching First Finger Backward)

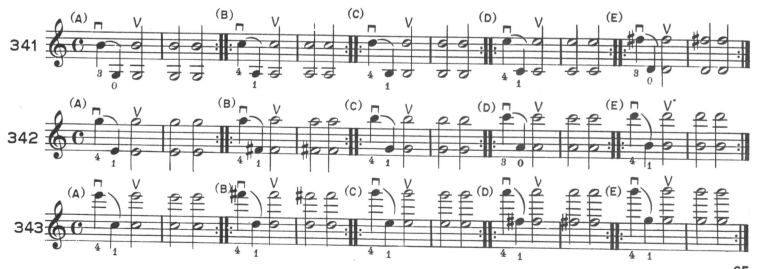

Etude in Tenths

De BERIOT

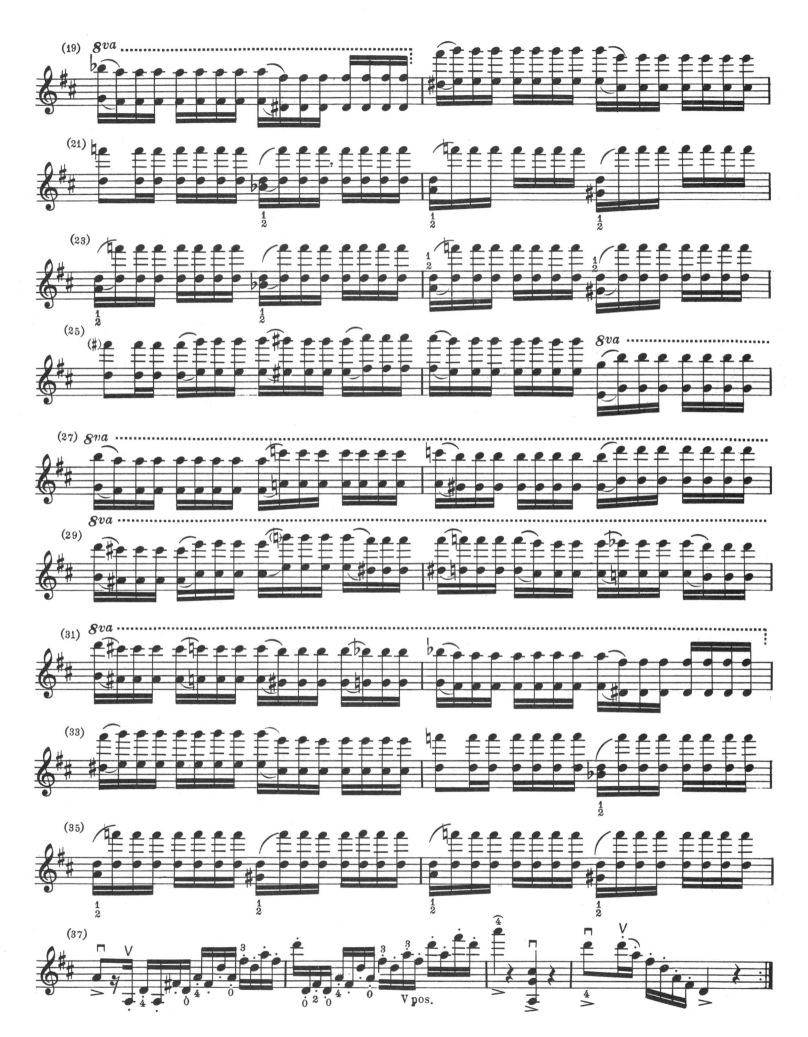

Introduction to Scales in Tenths

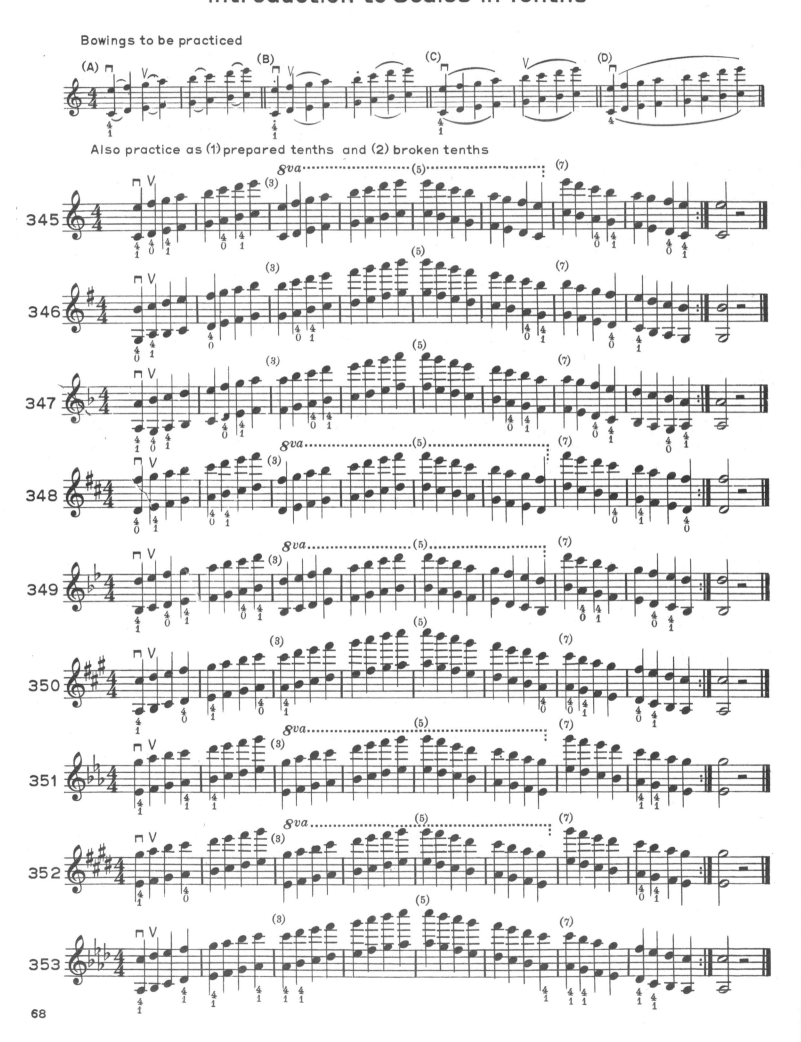

Etude d'Artiste
(Chromatic Thirds and Octaves)

De BERIOT

Advanced Chord Exercises in Major Keys

De BERIOT

Advanced Chord Exercises in Minor Keys

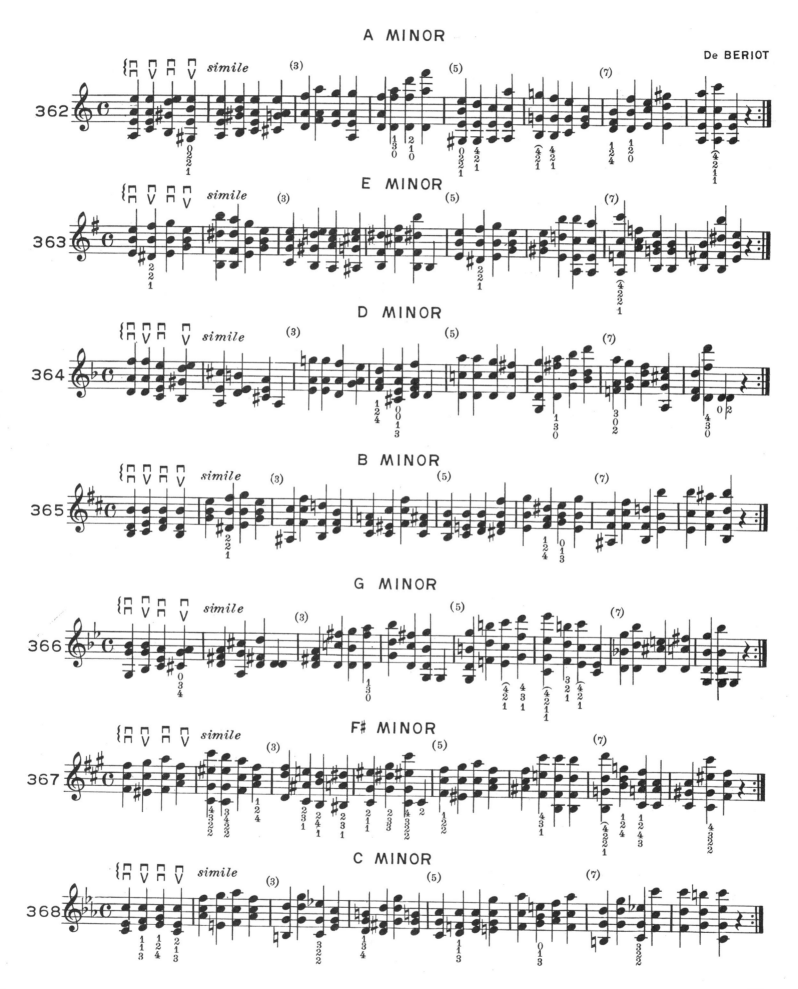

Chromatic Fantasy

De BERIOT

369